As the Image of God, You Have Worth

by

Kevin Dewayne Hughes

Cover Photo: Paradise in the Philippines.

Title Photo: The sun setting over the bay in the Philippines.

Back Photo: The jungle in the Philippines.

Photography by
Kimberly Monteclaro Hughes

Kimberly is the wife of the author and assists him in modeling and photography.

Christian Warrior Arts Association

As the Image of God, You Have Worth

by
Kevin Dewayne Hughes

Published by
Ace Kiwami Publications

Edition
First

Dedication

To everyone, everywhere. You have much worth and I send love to all of you.

Acknowledgements

Yeshua (Jesus)

It is through a relationship with the Messiah that I came to understand love for all living things.

Table of Contents

Forward
Steve Hackman

I had low self-esteem and I was under constant assault on social media. I couldn't get a break. Constant depression flooded my minds.

Kevin Dewayne Hughes came along on TikTok with his @Troll.Fighter account, and took on some of my trolls. He inspired me and gave me hope. Then I saw some of his other TikTok accounts. He was a man to aspire to be like.

I started following his advice and motivational messages and I changed. My depression lessened and I started to feel good about myself. I now take on the trolls and I will send trolls to @troll.fighter.

Kevin Dewayne Hughes presents motivational messages that have helped me and I know they will help you too.

9

Steve Hackman
Texas
USA
15 January 2023

Preface

The present text is filled with daily motivational messages for use in telling you that you have worth beyond what anyone can tell you.

I grew up thinking I was ugly and stupid due to constant bullying. As time went on, I accepted Jesus as my Lord and Savior and He changed me. I came to realize that I was neither ugly nor was I stupid.

This realize was manifested by the fact that I was the top performer in my college and university studies. I only did poorly in primary and secondary school because my self-esteem was low due to constant bullying. So I put no effort into being good at schooling.

I also noticed that women treated me a certain way. My self-esteem was low and my self-image was of a guy too ugly to be attractive to women. So I thought their messages were anything but sexual interest in me. After accepting Christ, I came to the realization that women in general were attracted to me; that their actions had always been the actions of a sexually interested woman.

Bullying is a horrible practice. Trolling is too, which is just a word bullies like to call themselves so they don't wear the bully label.

I have vowed to do two things with my life in service to God. One is to confront the evils of trolling and bullying head on. The other is to help the victims of bullying and trolling to realize their true selves and true potential. The distortions that bullies and trolls present about a person can destroy a person's life.

Kevin Dewayne Hughes
Tenkidokan
Kancho
Bad-As, Surigao Del Norte
26 January 2023

Introduction

We can all reprogram and rewire our brains. Sometimes we have low self-esteem, poor self-image, low self-confidence, and low self-worth. These were programmed and wired and they can be reprogrammed and rewired.

The key is to meditate and visualize the things you want to be true about yours. Then engage is study and training to help realize the new you. The training and study feeds back into the mediation and belief is created. When you believe the new you is now you really are, then the reprogramming and rewiring is complete.

This text is to help people rewire and reprogram their self-image, self-worth, and self-esteem. Start with day one. Recite the daily mantra several times to yourself. Then read the normal print text. Repeat the mantra to yourself throughout the day. Start to see yourself as the bolded text presents. The next day, do the same with the following day's text.

When you hit the final day, feel free to return to day one and start the process over. If you need to repeat a day, then please do so. This is a one week course and should be repeated many times.

It is my hopes to help as many people to realize that they are worth far more than they realize.

Please feel free to use the blank spaces to take journal notes for the day. Record how you feel. Write down some thoughts. Use this information to see how you have change over time.

Day 1

You are created in the very image of the prefect God.

God is flawless. Like a perfect gem stone has great value, you too have great value. And the image of God has more value than any gem stone. You are precious.

Mantra: **I am created in the image of the Creator God.**

17

Day 2

You offer something unique that no one else can offer.

You may engage in activities that others engage in. But your personality, behaviors, mindset, and several other things are unique to you. You off this richness to the world around you and only you can offer you.

Mantra: **I am unique and valuable**

19

Day 3

I and others love you.

God is love. He wants us to love each other. This is unconditional love. I don't care what you look like or what you have done. I and others like me love you with Godly love.

Mantra: **I am loved by others**

.

Day 4

You are stronger than you think and definitely stronger than what others think.

Strength is of many forms. You can be physically, mentally, emotionally, and spiritually strong. And there are various strengths within each of those. You are stronger in one or more of these.

Mantra: **I am strong**

23

Day 5

You have valuable talents to offer the world.

Talents can range just like strengths can. You may not see your talents now, but they are there. You may not see their worth, but your talents do have value.

Mantra: **I am talented.**

25

Day 6

You are bright and intelligent.

There are multiple intelligences. Unfortunately, IQ is only a measure of academical intelligence. You have high IQ in one or more of the various intelligences.

Mantra: **I am smart.**

27

Day 7

You matter to me and others.

Everything that makes you who you are is special and matters to me and people like me. We want to see you succeed and become the best version of you possible.

Mantra: **I matter.**

Concluding Remarks

Be sure to use the blank pages to journal your progress in rewiring and reprogramming your self-image, self-esteem, self-worth, and self-confidence.

I hope to see the new image of you shinning brightly.

Thank you for reading.

Kevin Dewayne Hughes
Christian Warrior Arts Association
Founder
Bad-As, Surigao Del Norte
Philippines
27 January 2023

Afterword
Maurice Kirkpatrick

I was suicidal from all the trolling I got. I just couldn't take it.

Kevin Dewayne Hughes came along on Facebook and gave me a new outlook. I used the mantra in this text and I am a different person. I no longer let the trolls get to me.

Maurice Kirkpatrick
Texas
USA
26 January 2023

About the Author

Kevin Dewayne Hughes

Kevin is the founder of the Christian Warrior Arts Association and is also the founder the Tenkidokan school. He holds degrees, qualifications, and recognitions in martial arts, energy arts, fitness, science, engineering, and theology.

He lives in the Philippines as an expat with his wife and Fil-Am son. His activity in the Philippines and his marriage have caused many to seek his advice on both living in the Philippines and on finding love.

33

About the Organization

Christian Warrior Arts Association

The Christian Warrior Arts Association was founded by Kevin Dewayne Hughes with the purpose of certifying martial arts teachers who teach martial arts free of religion. That is to be Christian friendly. It was not purposed to certify Christian martial artists only.

Its other function is spreading the Gospel of Christ.

Over time, the Christian Warrior Arts Association has grown. The Institute for Advanced Christian Studies was formed to explore topics from the apocryphal writings, Jewish literature, and other sources. These other sources are not studied as Scriptures but as a look into the various mind sets that have existed in the Abrahamic religions.

The Knights of Polaris is another sub organization that emerged as a charitable arm or arm of servitude to help better society.

Suggested Reading

Title: Introduction to the Theory of Yin-Yang
Edition: 2nd
Author: Kevin Dewayne Hughes
Publisher: Ace Kiwami Publications
Year: 2020
ASIN: B08DBY32TX
ISBN: 979-8667867869

This book treats yin and yang as a scientific theory of how the universe works. Its principles are then presented as a means to manage and live a better life.

Other Books By
Ace Kiwami Publications

Title: Martial Arts Philosophy and Wisdom: Proverbs, Sayings, and Quotes Used in Martial Arts

Edition: 1st

Author: Kevin Dewayne Hughes

Date: 2022

ASIN: B0BRDPJXH7

ISBN: 979-8371234612

Title: New Age Science: The Greek Zodiac - Aries

Edition: 1st

Author: Todd Johnson

Date: 2020

ASIN: B08DC1Z8ND

ISBN: 979-8668435234

Title: The Blind Faith of Militant Atheism
Edition: 1st
Author: Kevin Dewayne Hughes
Date: 2023
ASIN: B0BRYZP95Y
ISBN: 979-8373178907

Title: How to Punch Faster
Edition: 1st
Author: Kevin Dewayne Hughes
Date: 2023
ASIN: B0BRZ4GBPG
ISBN: 979-8373188166

Title: The Importance of Wealth
Edition: 1st
Author: Amy Smith
Date: 2023
ASIN: B0BRYF3FFP

Short
About Author

Kevin Dewayne Hughes

He is the founder of the Christian Warrior Arts Association and gives motivation messages to people while fighting bullies and trolls.

Short
Book Description

Mantra to change your self-image, self-esteem, self-worth, and self-confidence are given. Instructions in use as well as information on each mantra, are presented.

Christian Warrior Arts Association

Published By: Ace Kiwami Publications

Social Media

TikTok Handles

@kevkimhughes

Primary content is on living in the Philippines.

***

@tenkidokan

Primary content is martial arts.

***

@cwaassoc

Primary content is Christian related. This is the channel for the Christian Warrior Arts Association.

Increasing
Speed and
Power the
Tai Chi Way
Kevin Dewayne Hughes